Summer '20

Kanishkaa Seerangan

BookLeaf Publishing

Presentation by *BookLeaf Publishing*

Web: www.bookleafpub.com

E-mail: info@bookleafpub.com

ISBN: 9789358369052

First edition 2023

DEDICATION

To my closest confidants, the five of you,
who've shaped me into who I am as a person.
It's more than blood that bonds us all.

ACKNOWLEDGEMENT

It isn't my favourite season, by any means, but summers have always brought this unmistakable sense of nostalgia to me. The feeling of hot sand under your feet, wet shorts from wading into the water, and the sweet scent of ice cream resurfaces childhood memories that I have no hope of burying. The second we cross the last day of June off our calendars and flip to July is the second it all starts to come back to me; images flashing through my head like scenes from a movie. Biking with my friends. Climbing trees together. Late night walks around the city. But then I start to realize that all of these memories have one thing in common: my best friends, who mean the world to me. I wouldn't be here without them, so thank you so, so much. I lub ju all! To my teachers as well, who have never failed to call on me to share my stories aloud to the class during our creative writing hour, even though I never raised my hand. I'm grateful for all your support and encouragement, even if it did compel me to step out of my comfort zone a little. I'll never forget what my teacher said to me when handing me the Language Arts award during my eighth grade graduation, as the words "You're such a talented writer" have never been so inspiring to a thirteen-year-old. I have learned so much from my teachers, so thank you. And last, but certainly not the least, thank you to my family, who have been with me every step of the way. You are the reason I write, and my motivation behind each and every one of my pieces. I greatly appreciate everything you've done for me, which is pretty much everything. Without you, this book wouldn't have been possible, so thank you, everyone.

PREFACE

"In youth we learn; in age we understand."
- Marie von Ebner-Eschenbach

Summer '20

There were five of us, bright young things,
Always aching for more.
We called it Summer 13,
This was our year, the year we were together.

Always aching for more,
Bare feet running on sidewalks.
This was our summer together,
We were never enough for us.

Running barefoot on sidewalks,
Chasing under the blistering heat.
We were never enough for us,
Bikes racing each other, gaining speed.

We chase (for what?) till the end of day,
Sprint through streets downtown.
Our bikes race each other, we're gaining speed
Till we spot the cars speeding too.

Sprint through streets downtown,
While passing by the riverside.
Till we spot the cars speeding too,
Sneaking glances at bar couples.

While passing by the riverside,

We stop - one stop - and turn around.
Instead of sneaking glances at bar couples,
We see our future ahead of us.

We stop our only stop and turn around,
Eyes fixated on the water, glistening,
We see our future - our world - ahead of us,
Tall, bright, buildings; our next big step.

Eyes fixated on the water, glistening,
We finally turn away, in thought,
Of our next big steps, inside tall buildings,
And make our way in the afternoon sun.

After finally turning away, in thought
We indulge in A La Carte; gelato our escape.
And bathe our way in the afternoon's sun,
Tongues licking lips, cream trickling down.

Our A La Carte indulgence then escapes us,
When we eat too much, stomach stuffed.
Tongues licking cream trickling down lips,
A flyer flies by, and hits our chest.

When stomachs stuffed from eating,
We haul ourselves up.
Taking the flying flyer,
"Used Book Sale" something we needed.

We get up and bike all the way,
Passing the bridge, the clock, and the banner.
We need something from the "Used Book Sale"
Edde's Graffiti Alley thinks otherwise.

Passing the banner, the bridge, and the clock.
Detouring through Jackson Park,
Edde's Graffiti Alley is long gone,
But the lights from the Park will be here soon.

Detouring through Jackson Park,
"We're in a hurry, we're wasting time"
But the lights from the Park-
-I said not now, c'mon, let's go!

"We're in a hurry, we're wasting time"
So we finally arrive, in the nick of time.
"See, I told you, we're here now"
Now we wallow in pages, in words.

When we finally arrive, in the nick of time,
The librarian hands us the key.
Now we wallow in pages, in words,
As we lose ourselves, once again.

The key to freedom is in our hands
We flip through books,
And lose ourselves, like we did before,
But this time, we are smiling.

Flipping through books,
Carrying them in our arms,
And this time, we are smiling
As we bike home, arms occupied.

Carrying them in our arms,
We laugh to one another.
Our arms occupied, as we head home,
Gazing at the sky.

We laugh to one another
With flushed faces; hair a mess,
Gazing at the sky
A pinkish, playful haze.

Messy hair and faces flushed,
At last, we return to our hill.
The sky, a pinkish, playful haze
Is a Van Gogh painting in itself.

At last, it is our hill we return to,
Laying down; the grass, our blanket.
A Van Gogh painting in itself,
The warm breeze of summer's night.

We lay down, the grass blanketing us,
Listening to nature's lullaby.
And summer's warm, night breeze,

Gently tucks us in; a final good night.

Listening to nature's lullaby,
This was the summer we turned 13.
Gently tucked in, a final good night,
We were five, bright, young things.

Barefoot

My key to feeling are my own two feet.
I touch, I feel, I sink, I stand my ground,
kicking off my shoes to feel the grass beneath
my toes,
the morning dew fresh against my feet

This feeling I get when my soles meet
pavement, the newfound awareness of rock, of
stone.
My soles are spotted with tiny, red dots
from stepping on pebbles that prickle my feet.

After my feet ache from rough concrete,
I sink them into the damp dirt around me, wet
with worms
and the moist morning air, thick and sweaty and
cool
and when i pull them out, dark brown outlines
my toenails.

The sun shines down in the afternoon, the heat
baking the sand and my feet alive, as I wriggle
my toes free
the grains of sand burying my ankles, each one a
tiny

scalding pinch against my already scalding feet.

Kicking off shoes i wade into the water, and
repeat
this process of feeling i have known for so long,
and drown
my feet into the pond, extinguishing a fire
burning inside of me,
sinking them to cool me,
sinking them to revive me

This key to feeling feels complete,
because every dip my toe takes,
is a new journey
a new path for me to take, one step at a time.

What it Means to Be Alive

Oh, I find this exhilarating
to catch a snake and run away from its fangs,
to run to the edge of tomorrow, racing against
your heartbeat, hearing the thrumming of your
blood flow in and out of your heart, your
speeding pulse breaking every limit you have set
for yourself.
The surge of adrenaline after every itch, every
tug, every nag you have to scream at the skies
above.
To shout like you may never shout again,
to yell at the top of your lungs just to hear the
sound of your voice to prove that you exist,
To take every breath like it's your last,
it's what gives meaning to the word "alive,"
the gods are what give us life.
Yet they are more dead than ever,
for they have never really lived, just merely
existed.

Summer Rewind

rewind to summer '20

when sky blue jean jackets were all the rage
when we scraped hubba bubba off the soles of
our vans
when our minds and words were well beyond
our age
when we had sticky popsicle lips and chalk dust
hands

rewind to summer '20

when we slept under the shade of the sugar
maple trees
when we brushed aside the warnings of our
parents
when our cheeks felt the tickle of a soft, summer
breeze
when pool parties were thrown while running
errands

rewind to summer '20

when we believed we could get anywhere with
only our bikes

when ten extra minutes meant a ticket to
paradise
when we stole glances at passerby's and talked
about types
when we bulk-bought candy and thought less
about the price

rewind to summer '20

when time and tide always waited for little kids
like me
when young wasn't always the same thing as
youth
when the only hurt we experienced were scraped
arms and knees
when our lunch boxes consisted of freshly sliced
fruit

take me back to summer '20
take me way back
when

when you and me believed that this would last
forever
without a sliver of doubt

Bring Me Home

summers back home were an experience of its
kind
it's not something I can just expect you to
understand by reading about it
or by writing to you about it
or even by telling you about it, because I don't
know if I can just
capture the way the sun's rays shone down upon
us when we ran across open, grassy fields,
or the sounds of the bustling city, lively and
vibrant early in the mornings,
already filled with people going places and cars
taking them there, and you wouldn't believe the
unbelievably hot afternoons, the blistering heat
enough to dry sand itself, with the sun high in
the sky and us wandering around in our house,
fanning ourselves with books and eating
watermelons to stay alive, and you wouldn't
have witnessed the desperation in our voices and
minds and bodies, tugging at us to get up and
run somewhere
 and I'm not sure if you'd feel the
overwhelming touch in your heart that pulls at
you

when you realize it's the only place you'll want
to be in
it's the only place you'll ever call home
it's not enough for you to listen to me
I need to show you these things
I need to bring you home
bring me home

Routine

I get up, no later than 6
(it gets pretty bright at 6)
and I leave a note for my parents
hopping on my bike, I start a journey to
somewhere.

Awkward Teenage Phase

when the young gooselings grow into their
in-between stage
their mothers, once so protective, watch them go
and so they finally reach their awkward teenage
phase

they eye the world from their mother's lenses, a
cage
between them and their sole interests, you know
when the young gooselings grow into their
in-between stage

they practice and perfect their mother's fiercest
gaze
holding it to her when honking, expressions' an
explicit "NO"
and so they finally reach their awkward teenage
phase

sometimes, when things get tough, they go off in
a rampage
filled to the brim with unspoken thoughts that
finally show
when the young gooselings grow into their
in-between stage

when this happens, they stop honking for days
but their mothers would be there to calm the
tantrums they'd throw
and so they finally reach their awkward teenage
phase

ah, the milestones and marks of such a fun age
they finally find their own wings, soaring as the
wind blows
when the young gooselings grow into their
in-between stage
and so they finally reach their awkward teenage
phase

Every Single One

what made it home was the people
the people I grew up with
those who taught me, and fought with me
who raised me and praised me
and who never failed to amaze me
the old, with warnings I dismissed with a hand
the young, with vigor I watched with intrigue
those who I saw every second of the day
and those who I've only seen for a second
those who've stuck by me, through the years
and those who I've left behind and lost
the ones who've supported my every decision
and the ones who didn't and still stood with me
I lived and loved and laughed
with every single one of them

What Matters To Us

sometimes i feel so small
too small to be daring
too small to believe i can make a difference

we think we're so important
because we are, but only to us
in fifty years, nothing we did
nothing we felt
nothing we experienced
none of it will change anything

we live in our own little world of make-believe
playing pretend because it

we spend so much time thinking about what
matters to us
yet we don't realize that we're the only ones that
do

Make-Believe Worlds

we knew what we were doing, most of the time
we knew what we felt
we knew we weren't alone
so then tell me, why

when the moon, so brilliant, finally dips into the
water
meeting its scintillating reflection
saying goodbye to the stars above
why do we feel that a tiny piece of ourselves
dissipates when we realize
the day has ended it's very last minute?

our fear that the stars themselves may be blotted
out
and nothing is left for us in the sky
nothing is left for tomorrow
when tomorrow will always come by
we forget that, sometimes
and we think it might not happen
we think we won't get a second chance
because when we see the end of something
we end a part of ourselves, too
and understand that in advance

but each night comes another day
each day comes a new dawn
a new beginning
the birth of something new
another chance to make mistakes
break promises
and fix them all again
under the orange blush of sunrise
after an empty, desolate midnight

we thrived in our make-believe worlds
living our make-believe life
feeling as real as we really are
being as full as we can possibly be

For The Very Last Time

Life is a funny thing, really.
It's like a train station
with people coming in and out of every stop.

The summer we were kids, we ran and told lies
to our mothers and fathers who caught our every
line,
so we took our road to freedom and snuck out at
night.

This was the summer we defined the letter "I"
The summer we were kids for the very last time.

Time Flies

We grew up too fast.
(that summer we were kids for the last time.)
It's the truth, and it hurts
when you realize,
those eighteen years of childhood
flew by in twelve.
Just twelve mere years of endless possibilities
and second chances.
Just twelve, trifling years of love and laughter
and illimitable dreams we thought would
happen,
because we believed they would.
We really believed it.

Let there be a seed
planted inside my skin
let it soothe my scars
let it seal the crevices
and heal what never is mending
what soon will be ending.

Let there be a spark
ignited from my soul
let it shine brighter
let it glow under my dismay

like snow on a holiday
melting, what soon will go away.

Cloudgazing

Summer days with just a soft breeze
that tickled the long blades of grass.
The wind whistling through the branches
of tall oak trees that loomed over us,
sheltering us from the sun's glare,
as we lie in the shade, keeping us cool
from the blistering heat of afternoons.

When the sun shines high
at the tip of the sky,
we watch the clouds drift
by us, so when we can, we try
naming them, shape-shifting from

Soft, fuzzy brush strokes
to heavy, billowing orbs,
the faint wisps of feathery, balmy milk
the snow-like hues of cotton-candy clouds,
puffy and light with a lemon outline,
the touch of sunlight bordering the edges,
creating distinctive shapes with our imaginations
as hazy as they were,
as lazy as we seemed
killing time with our weapons of naivety
so good as it felt

searching for patterns in the sky,
lying on the ground in the middle of July.

Even if none of it will matter,
it still holds value.
These are memories worth keeping.

Wait For Me

Home
not where I live
or where I go
but where I love
and where I hope
a place where I write my path
and everyone else does too
a place where I feel safe
and full of the people I love
and want to see myself around
every step along the way
where I thrive
and where I express myself
where I wake up feeling loved and appreciated
and I fall asleep feeling the same
a place full of its own imperfections
and knots of human nature
where I see myself with all of you
wait for me
I'm coming home.

Summer Nights

Summer nights in the city,
lying under the astonishing view of the stars,
delightful young dreams that hinder our
thoughts.

City lights, so picturesque,
under tall buildings, towering over us.
We're a silhouette in the moonlight,
the warmth of the evening summer breeze
surround us,
taking us into a soft embrace,
tickling our skin
planting kisses in our hair,
as the sun sets across the horizon
and the sky sinks deep into an obscurity.

Night falls upon us,
and the belle of twilight comes into view.
The stars float across the brilliance of the moon,
dancing in a crevasse of emptiness

Time Feels Funny

Flashes of summer
when the weeks blend together
and we forget what day it is.
Time feels funny
because it doesn't work like it used to.
We've abandoned order,
we've abandoned time,
turning to the sun and the stars for help,
giving us a new way of life
knocking some sense into our brains,
our boundless, cosmic minds.

Live to Love

I live with you
I laughed with you
I cried with you
I smiled with you
I scowled with you
I sang with you
I danced with you
I fought with you
I grieved with you
I love all of you
After all, live is only a letter away from love.

Main Character

We talked about our lives like a movie scene,
And we're the part everyone's been talking
about.
Always the main characters,
This was our show.
And we were the stars of it all.

Perfect Little Imperfections

Our perfect little imperfections,
our scars we used to hide behind our smiles,
tears we used to cover up with a laugh.
Choke back a sob and put on a show,
for everyone to watch
so no one will know.
Our pretty little myths
Hiding what can't be shown.

More Than Blood

We've shared mothers,
And brothers,
And grandparents too, I'm sure of it.
We were made of each other.
It's more than blood that bonds,
It's family.

Goodbye

i'll never say it
i'll never say it
i won't
i won't
i won't
you'll never hear it.

9 789358 369052